Focus *grid, colwell*

The Game of Grids

Kylie Colwell

Author
    Kylie Colwell

Coordinator of the *focus* series and Professor of Design
    Sarah McDowell

Editing Support
    Leah Vaught

Special Thanks
    Geoff Newton for initiating the "*focus* series"
    Don Adelta for sharing the *focus* series concept
    Leah Vaught and Rene Toncar for proving props
    Ken Colwell for providing camera

Photography
    Vecteezy.com, Freepik.com, PressureUA, Josh Withers,
    Bruno Cantuaria, Ozan Culha, Cerro_photography, Vicnt,
    KoolShooters, Atypeek Dgn, Cottonbro Studio

Layout
    Typeset in Adobe Garamond Pro Regular and *Italic*
    File created with Adobe InDesign CC

Print
    Printing by Lulu Press Inc.
    Cover 100 lb. laminated cover stock. Text: 80l lb.

Edition Draft
    This edition was created in order to document the extent
    of research produced during the 2023 fall semester of the
    junior level BFA Graphic Design course at Ohio University.
    This was produced and distributed through Lulu Press, Inc.
    as a vehicle for additional research and discussion beyond
    course requirements.

ISBN 978-1-304-89076-4

Table *of contents*

01 | THE STUDY

WHAT'S A GRID?

Grids are all around us. Everyday we see and use grids, whether consciously or
unconsciously. While grids can be used to confine, they can also be used as a
guide for how to 'break' space. In this study of grids, I aimed to explore both
of these usages. I began by creating 20 unique grids, then selecting one to be
manipulated in 20 different ways, with 6 iterations of each manipulation. The
initial grids would form my structure, that then could be broken throughout
the manipulation process. The final result would be over 120 different grids.

Before beginning any project, first you must define the perimeters and
your goals. In this study, a grid was defined as singular object or form
repeated horizontally and vertically within a square. The columns and
rows should consist of 10-16 units in order to ensure the grid is the
proper size for the manipulation phase of the study. Working within these
confines and in large quantities will force creative breakthroughs.

INITIAL GRIDS

When creating my initial 20 grids, I tried to create a wide variety of forms. Some of these were basic shapes, like circles and triangles, while other became very complex forms. On the right is a sample of 16 of the grids created during this portion of the study.

Certain shapes and qualities I found more appealing than others. I was drawn toward grids that created interesting forms in the negative space. I enjoyed the idea that a simple inversion could create such a dramatic change to the overall effect of the piece. I also found myself more interested in the more complex forms I was creating, however I knew that the more simple forms would allow for a greater variety of manipulation in the coming phases of the study. When selecting the final grid I would utilize throughout the manipulation process, I wanted to choose a grid which represented these factors that I was drawn to, and had a balance of complexity and simplicity.

MANIP-ULATION

The grid seen below is an example of a manipulation of the base grid. I explored many different forms of manipulation throughout this process, from gradients, to slicing, to warping, and more. In this manipulation, I simple cut off half of the star diagonally, creating rows of pointed polygons.

BASE GRID

The grid seen above was selected to be utilized throughout the manipulation process. This grid consists of a repeated four-pointed star. I found this grid to be the perfect balance of a simplistic base shape with interesting negative space, and many opportunities for interesting manipulations.

RESULT

The manipulation process yielded 120 different grids, each being completely unique. I found interest in how varied of an effect I could create within iterations of the same manipulation. As seen on this page, there is a great variety that can be created, even through the most basic of manipulation.

ITERATIONS

These grids (above & right) are iterations of the manipulated grid (left). In the iteration seen above, I sliced the stars in half in a pattern to create a gradient effect. In the iteration seen to the right, I utilized the half stars to create a swirling pattern.

02 | THE APPLICATION

MIND MAP

Now that the grid study process has been completed, I move into the second phase of this project: The Application. I was tasked with finding a way to integrate the grids I had created throughout the grid study into a design process, whether functionally or conceptually. Prior to the design portion of the project, I had to conduct research to solidify a concept.

The first step in my research process was to create a mind map. A mind map is a form of brainstorming consisting of placing one central idea in the middle of a page, then creating branches of related feelings, objects, or concepts. The free-form nature of mind mapping allowed me to open up my mind and explore ideas for an application of my grid. While I began with fairly straightforward or obvious concepts, as the map branches out the ideas become more and more creative.

After examining my mind map, I found the ideas and themes that I was drawn towards were entertainment, accessories, and home goods, and I knew I wanted to draw inspiration from the 1960s and 70s. Now that I had narrowed down the options, I moved on to visual research in hopes of finalizing my application selection.

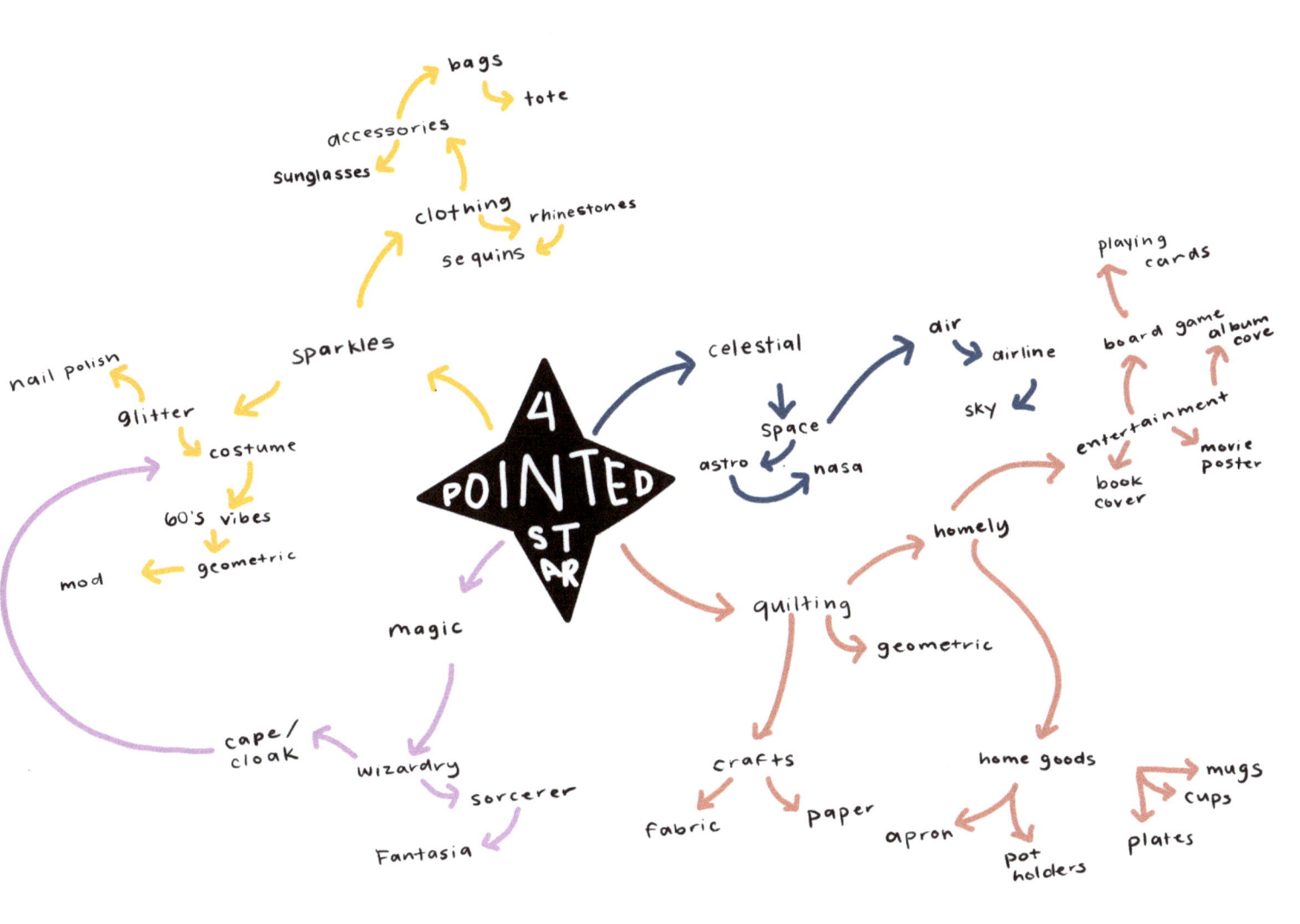

bags
tote
accessories
sunglasses
clothing
rhinestones
sequins
Sparkles
nail polish
glitter
costume
60's vibes
geometric
mod
magic
cape/cloak
wizardry
sorcerer
Fantasia

4 POINTED STAR

celestial
air
airline
sky
space
astro
nasa

playing cards
board game
album cove
entertainment
book cover
movie poster

homely
quilting
geometric
crafts
fabric
paper
home goods
apron
pot holders
mugs
cups
plates

VISUAL RESEARCH

In the visual research process, I searched the Internet for images that defined the aesthetic I was seeking to portray. I found images that had a 1960s or 70s aura. I also searched for images that reflected the themes of entertainment, accessories, and home goods.

By conducting visual research, I was able to clearly define the mood of my application as well as find inspiration. Creating a mood board through visual research allowed me to narrow down even further which application ideas I found myself drawn to visually.

APPLICATION

After conducting my research, I decided to apply my grids
to playing cards. I chose this application because of the
inherent grid-like nature of playing cards. Classic playing
card design utilizes a grid base for the card faces and in many
games, the cards are laid out in a grid. Playing cards, while
being functional, also lend themselves well to creative design
application, as there is room to customize the faces of the
cards, as well as the backs, and the box the deck comes in.

When you think of playing cards, you think of the Bicycle brand.
Traditional playing card brands such as Bicycle typically utilize a
limited color palette, with red and black being the primary colors
and blue and yellow utilized as accents. These cards have heavily
ornamented backs in one color and geometric illustrations for
the face cards. I drew inspiration from classic playing card design,
while also introducing a broader color palette and a more modern
design which utilizes my grids on the backs and faces of the cards.
Some descriptive characteristics I kept in mind while designing
this deck included crisp, colorful, funky, mod, and 1960s inspired.

The following pages show the brand guidelines I developed, the
final card and box designs, and photographs of the prototype.

BRAND GUIDELINES

Aa ABCDEFG HIJKLMN OPQRSTU VWXYZ

Breaker Slab Bold — Title Text

Aa ABCDEFG HIJKLMN OPQRSTU VWXYZ

Interstate Condensed Bold — Card Text

GAME OF GRIDS
PLAYING CARDS
52 CARD DECK

GAME OF GRIDS
PLAYING CARDS
52 CARD DECK

GAME OF GRIDS
PLAYING CARDS
52 CARD DECK

GAME OF GRIDS
PLAYING CARDS
52 CARD DECK

#88A649

#88A649

#A62051

#D9502F

#151940

#F29D52

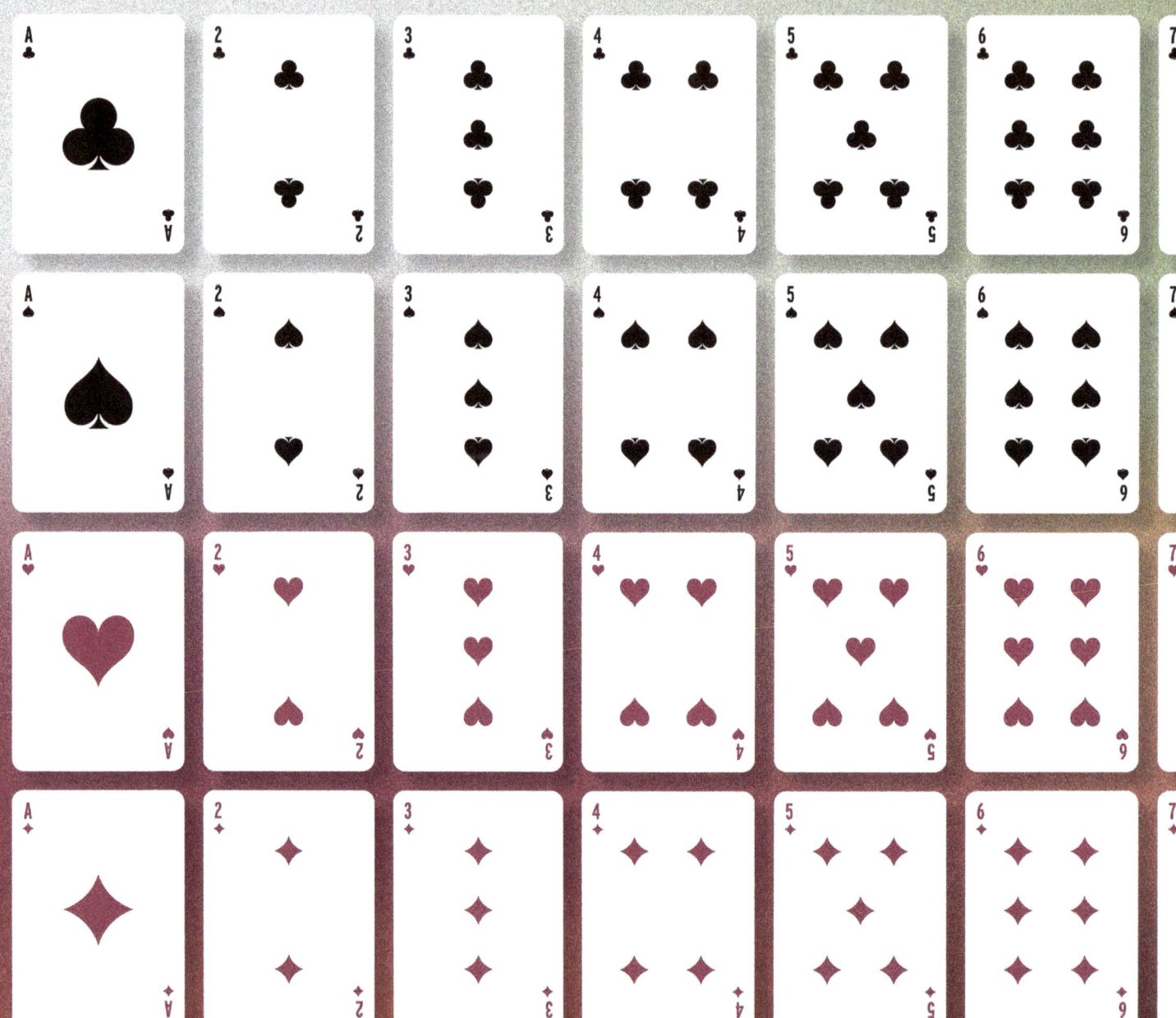

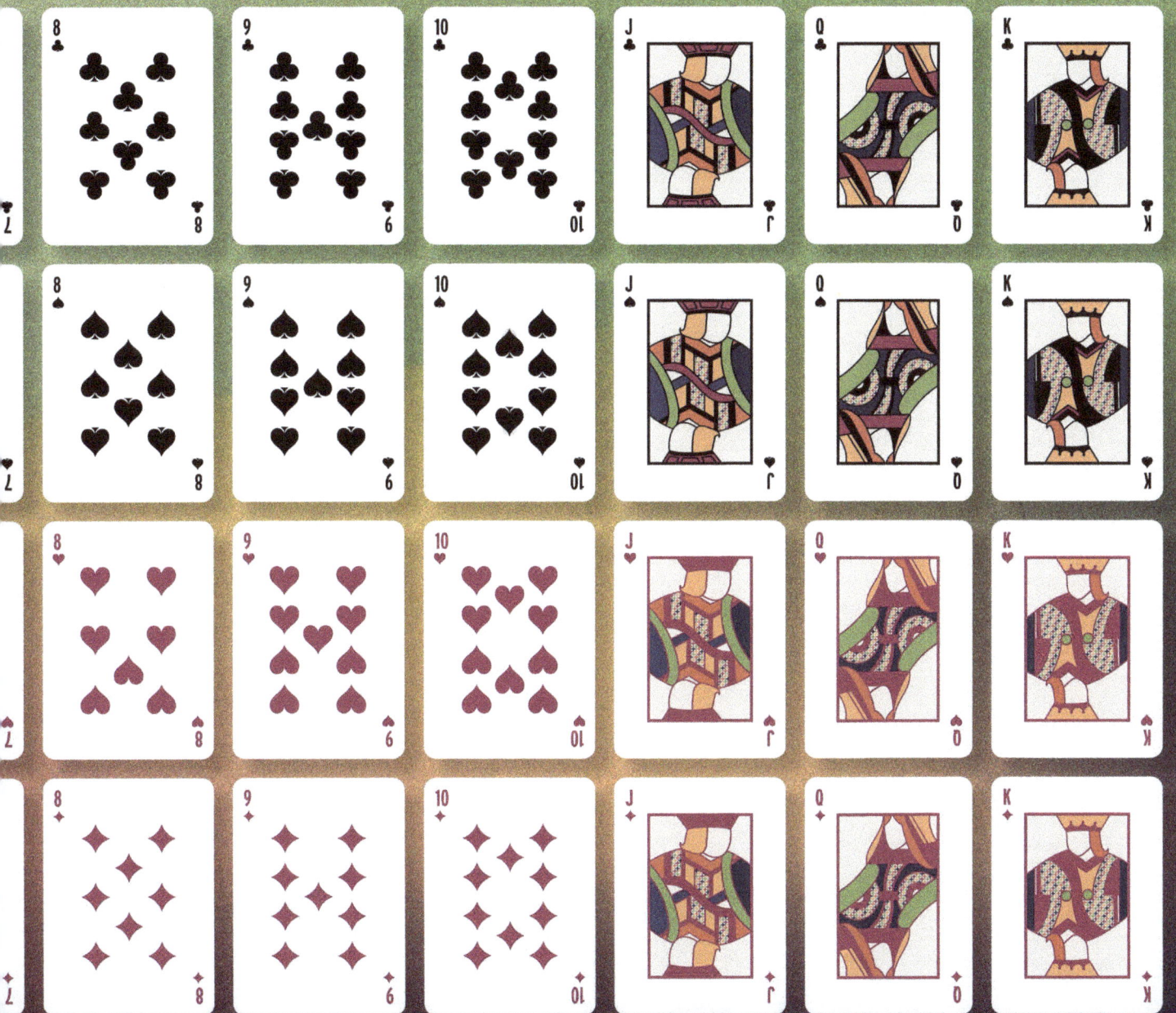

GAME OF GRIDS

PLAYING CARDS

52 CARD DECK

GAME OF GRID

PLAYING CARDS

52 CARD DECK

PLAYING CARDS

A

THE GAME OF GRIDS

In the beginning, I found the grid study process to be repetitive and daunting. However, I was shocked by how working in such a large quantity unlocked new levels of creativity, and was great practice in working quickly and within restrictions. This process taught me that your first idea isn't always the greatest, and that freely exploring many options is the best practice in creating.

As designers, we often are conducting studies, sketching, or making work that we don't believe will lead to anything. The application of this grid study shows that any idea can be turned into art, however abstract it may be. Never stop creating, as you never know where it may lead.

www.ingramcontent.com/pod-product-compliance
Lightning Source LLC
Chambersburg PA
CBHW041134280526
45792CB00014B/2415